# Ramblings of Blurose

NORA B. MONTGOMERY

Order this book online at www.trafford.com
or email orders@trafford.com

Most Trafford titles are also available at major online book retailers.

Print information available on the last page.

ISBN: 978-1-4669-6545-4 (sc)
ISBN: 978-1-4669-6544-7 (e)

*Trafford rev. 03/04/2017*

Trafford
PUBLISHING®   www.trafford.com
**North America & international**
toll-free: 1 888 232 4444 (USA & Canada)
fax: 812 355 4082

THIS IS LOVINGLY DEDICATED TO MY MOM, VEDA DECKER, HER
WRITING IS SOMETHING THAT I WILL ALWAYS REMEMBER.


THIS IS A COLLECTION OF MY WRITING OVER THE LAST FEW YEARS.
I AM PUTTING THEM TOGETHER FOR MY FAMILY AND FRIENDS. IT
IS MY HOPE THAT YOU WILL ENJOY READING THIS AS MUCH AS I
DID WRITING IT.

# Contents

# The Beast, Cancer

I COULD WIN THE NOBEL PRIZE IF I COULD PREVENT THE DEMISE OF ALL THE MANY FRIENDS WITH CANCER. FROM THE TINIEST MITES TO THE ONES OF GREAT HEIGHT THEY WOULD ALL WIN THE FIGHT WITH THE BEAST KNOWN AS CANCER.

GONE WOULD BE THE PLAGUE THAT SO MANY IN OUR AGE. IF ONLY IT COULD BE LOCKED IN A CAGE, NEVER TO MORE TO RAGE AND RAMPAGE. IT WOULD ONLY BE A WORD ON A PAGE THAT HISTORY WOULD ASK; WHAT WAS THAT WHICH TOOK SO MANY OF ALL AGES BACK IN THOSE DARK AGES?

MANY HAVE FOUGHT AND WON. OTHERS HAVE PUT UPA GREAT FIGHT ONLY TO BE STRUCK DOWN BY THIS MOST FEARED PEAST. SET US ALL RAISE A PRAYER AND THAT IT WILL SOON BE ANSWERED THAT SOON THERE WILL BE NO MORE CANCER.

# The Day Dream

THE DAY HAD BEEN LONG AND SUBJECTS A BORE. I SIT LOOKING OUT OF THE DUSTY, FINGERPRINTED DOOR. DEEP IN MY BRAIN COME A PICTURE OF A WATERFALL. IN THE POOL BELOW THE FALL, I SWIN TO THE BIRDCALL. I WAS FREE TO THE BOREDON AND IN MY FAVORITE PLACE. COULD THERE BE ANY WONDER THAT THIS WAS IN GOD'S GRACE. WITH THE RINGING OF THE BELL, I WAS SNAPPED BACK THE HOT CLASSROOM. I HAD A SMILE ON MY FACE BACAUSE I HAD ESCAPED. NOW I WAS BACK, BUT I KNEW QUIET PEACE.

# A Mother's Prayer

God, Bless the child at my breast. May it grow to know that it is loved with all there is in a mothers heart. May this child grow healthy, and with a good heart. May this child be caring of others and live a life full of wonders. May this child be filled with the knowledge that is there for all to learn and make the best of life.

As a mother, I wonder what this child will grow to be. Will it be a doctor caring for those in need, or an astronaut flung out among the stars, or a general worker that works for the good its family? What ever it may be, may it be satisfied and fulfilled in what ever it does.

Sleep well my little one and may your tomorrows be filled with joy and the bright shining hope of great love. May your future be all that a mother would wish for her child and much more besides.

I give this child to your care Lord. Amen

# Headaches

There are times when you just have to lay down to get rid of them. Then there are those that you can take a pill and they disappear. Some are nagging, they just lay there in your head not bad enough to make you sick, but enough to let you know that they are there. Then there are those that have your neck and back of your head hurting to the point you want to scream. There are the ones that sit behind your eyes and make your squint to see what you are doing. For those unlucky enough to have them, there are migraines, those headaches that feel like someone has taken a hatchet after half your head. Last but not least is the granddaddy of them all, the ones that feel like some one has a jackhammer going inside and make you loose anything you eat. Headaches, from the tiny naggers to the giant jackhammers, they all make you want to find some place to hide your eyes and get rid of them.

## Frustration

The daily life that we live is full of frustration. If it is not the kids asking for something to do, it is the cat knocking over the plants. Then, there is always the problem of to many bills and not enough money to go around. There are all of the things that keep you running around in circles. Shopping to do; the kids to take to their different practices, the never ending job of keeping the house in some semblance of order. Not to be left out, there is the time that your spend trying to plan what to feed your bunch. That leaves little or no time for you, and what makes your feel like you matter. Truly this is just life, but do we have to have so much frustration?

# One Little Wish

If I had but one little wish, it would be that you were for me. Your eyes so blue would only see the love inside of me. The smile on your lips and their touch would only be for me. Your hands so strong would be gentle as they held mine. Yes, my one little wish would be for you to love me.

# Unusual Summer

The weather this summer has been very cool for this time of year. Nights that have been cool enough that you did not have to run the air conditioner. Days that were only in the upper eighties or lower nineties. With rain that fell just when the ground really needed the moisture. Yes, this has been an unusual summer. Usually by this time of summer, the grass is turning to a sick yellow from lack of water. The crops are turning brown for want of rain. The children look like lobsters or brown raisins from the son. Not this year. The grass is green; the crops are green and abundant; and the children are just a pleasant tan. The ponds are full of water and the world around us is pleasant to the eye. Thank God this has been a very comfortable summer.

# If Dogs Could Talk

What would happen if dogs could talk? Would there be as much abuse of small animals and children? Would there be as many crooks go uncaught, if dogs could talk? Would there be as many people that get by with crime if dogs could talk? Would we want to have as many unwanted dogs around if dogs could talk? Aren't we glad that dogs can't talk?

# An Anniversary Wish

Messages sent by card and by phone come your way on this, your special day. Thoughts of love and care are sent your way from those your touched in your life. Family and friends share the joy of another year spent together. Whether it has been one or ninety spent in the arms of the one you love. Wishes of continued joy and happiness come your way from all around you. Through times of tears and sadness remember the days of gladness. Your lives will always be filled with the blessings of having one another to love and cherish as the years go by. May there be many of them.

Some times it seems that the only prayers that are answered are the small ones that your put in as an after thought to the big things that you pray for. They are the ones that you almost don't think about asking for. We seem to always want more than we truly need or have room for in our lives. We need to stop and think before we go to our master to ask for things that we truly do not need but only want because of the pressures of the outside world. For the many truly wonderful things that we are given: family; friends; the fact that we are healthy; have food to eat, and a roof over our heads. We forget that there are many, even right here in our own country, who go without any of these things. So, as we go into the holiday season let us remember that it is the small prayers that are answered and to not be greedy in wanting the big things in life.

# Tough Questions

Things that had been on her mind and in her heart. The one questions that she needed answered was, why was her skin darker than that of her family? Why did she have a different color eyes than they had? Was there something that they had not told her about herself? Burning questions in a young girls mind.

Momma, please tell me the answers to my questions, for I need to know why I am different.

Looking into the sad eyes of her daughter, and with a lump in her throat, the mother answered.

Darling, you are the product of a mothers love and a love that could never be. I was young and he was going away to war never to return. The day I knew your were on the way, I got the news that your daddy had been killed in action and would never know that he was to be a father. A few short months later, I met your dad and got married and he has raised you like his own. That is why our look different from the rest of the family. But darling, never think that your are not part of this family for without you, my life would be missing a big piece. You are all I have left of my first love. My golden ray of sunshine, and the silver lining to the grey clouds in my past. I love you.

# Only A Father's Love

In the heart of a young girl there is only one real man in her life, that is her Father. She looks up to him for love and guidance throughout her young life. He is the measuring stick for all the young men that will come into her life want to share part of her time. Even when she is and adult, married and has a family of her own, there is still nothing like Her Father's Love. No other person can ever take his place or give her the same counsel. In her heart, his place has the most space because of the time she has spent with him. In time of trials it is his wisdom that she seeks, asking questions that are sometimes hard to ask. It matters not that they are miles apart, it is his words of encouragement and pride that lift her heart. Knowing that she has made him proud of her fills her heart with joy.

When in later years, she sits and listens to stories that she has heard a few hundred times, there is still a glow of love in her eyes that only happens in his presence. For only a fathers love can fill that special place in her heart. When that sad day comes that he is no longer there to tell the stories and make her smile, there is a hole that can never be patched in the tapestry of her life. For only a Father's love can fill the place that is now bare. Even when she knows that he is in a better place, it is only through the grace of another Father that she can make it through the tears.

# Lost To Soon

The animal world lost a great champion this week and the world lost a fine young man. Steve Erwin, known as the Crocodile Hunter, lost his life doing what he did best: being with wild animals. Swimming with stingrays on the coast of Australia, telling the word about the animals of the ocean, and giving the people the wonders of the under water world.

Lost to his loving family was this funny animal lover, that through TV had entertained us. We will all miss his energetic and passionate way of explaining about the animals of the world. From the smallest to the largest the animals seemed to know that Steve was their friend and would not hurt them. Even when they were in his hands, they seemed to embrace him and show that they understood that he was their friend. On land or at sea, Steve was always excited to show the world the animals that he found and encouraged us to keep the animals safe and to help keep them healthy for our children and grandchildren.

Our hearts go out to Teri, Bendi and Little Bob with the prayer that they will carry on and keep Steve's memories close. Gone but not forgotten to the world of fans, both human and animal. May God bless you and keep you Steve.

# Lonely Is The Way

Many sit in their living rooms looking through the window and dream of days gone by. Often, they wish that someone would come and see them and keep them company for a few minutes to break up the lonely hours of the day. Their children are busy with their own families and they don't seem to have time for their parents.

Lonely is the way of the ones that are getting older and don't get out as much as years gone by. Time passes slowly as the clock ticks off the hours, days, months, and years. Then again, the years pass so fast that it seems, like only a few days ago their young ones were being sent off to school and heading out on dates. Now, there is only a pet for company and maybe a friend stops by once and a while.

Not only do older people feel the loneliness of days spent alone. There are many that have disabilities that spend many days alone with no one to talk to or spend time with. Lonely is their way.

There is one that gives us his time and has sent us one that will listen to us as we sit in that lonely room. That is our Lord God. He has not forgotten us and we look up to him for comfort. We all need his gentle hand and guidance. For he too knows that lonely way just like you.

# The Summer Storm

The late August sky in the southwest was growing darker as the afternoon sun beat down on the dry parched earth. The grass had turned from the green to a soft yellow-gold. Sweat beaded up on the young girls brow as she played in the shade of the old maple tree in the yard. Mother had lemonade in a pitcher on the porch for her to drink. Off in the distance you could see the jagged streaks of lightning flashing to the ground followed by the deep rumble of the thunder. As she looked across the field, she could see the hot shimmering dance of the heat coming off the sun parched land. The hot breeze that was blowing made the grass move like the waves of the ocean coming on the shore.

As the storm clouds came closer, they looked as if they were tumbling over themselves as they raced across the sky. The lightning did a streaked dance across the clouds and the thunder sounded like an old wagon on a rough road. Promising a much needed rain that had been long in coming. Unaware of the weather changing around her, the child played on. She walked out into the grass following a butterfly, as the first big drops started to fall, slowly making circles in the dust that covered the ground. The rumble of the thunder became closer sounding like the deep base roll of the kettle drum and the rain drops started coming down faster and smaller. Until they were like small stinging points as they contacted the child's skin. Soon, the child was soaked and streams of water ran down her legs forming puddles at her feet.

Her mother calls her in out of the rain as the clouds tumble and roll across the sky. With lightning flashing its blue-white streaks along the ground. There is a resounding crack and the deep window rattling roar of thunder, the storm rages on.

Mother and child watch the rain as it washes across the window panes. There is no fear, only gladness that the rain has come to make the grass turn green again and give the lakes and ponds much needed filling. Now, there will be water for the animals and food for them to eat.

# The Shy Candle

On Sunday as church was starting, the youth were lighting the candles. But one of the candles was shy and seemed afraid to be lit and let its light shine. The youth went back a second time. This time the shy candle lit but its flame was very small. Little by little the flame became lager and the candle became brighter and brighter.

This is not unlike many Christians, myself included. We have been lit by the love of our savior but are shy about letting our light shine out in the world. Some of us are people that have many talents, yet we do not show those talents to the world. We keep them to ourselves and do not share them with others. Yet others have few talents, but cannot help but share the ones they have and are brightly shining for the Lord.

I was twelve when I first became a Christian and was baptized. I was so happy that I was glowing, but as I grew up my bright glow became just a small flame much like the candles. I felt shy when it came to showing my love for the Lord. It is not that I do not love him and worship him, it is just that I have a hard time opening up that part of me that is so personal to me. I seem to have many gifts that I can use in many ways, but it is very hard for me to let the inner light shine. For some that know me, you might think that I am fooling around with you, but it is true. My relationship with the Lord is very special and personal to me. When it comes down to sharing this with others I try to hide my little flame, I just can't seem to share what is so personal to me.

I grew up where there was a real rift in the home when it cane to religion. My father and my maternal grand mother were always fighting about what was right and wrong. Dad wanted us to go to church at the Baptist church and Grandma was a bible thumping Holiness and this was the problem. Two very strong willed people wanting their way and with two very different ways of worship. Mom was caught in the middle and took us kids to the Christian church. There, we found a peace that only lasted as long as we were there. Grandma would get us bible study papers form her church and read them to us when we were with her. It was very hard, to say the least, to be in that constant war of wills.

I learned to keep my thoughts to myself, and to keep the personal things locked away so that no one could hurt me with them. Like the little candle I do not want to let my light shine to brightly for fear of being noticed and open for hurt. This is one area of my life that I do not open up for anyone not even my husband. For me, my relationship with the Lord is personal and it is hard to share it at all.

Yes, with time I will let my light grow brighter, but I would need to have the support of my Christian friends and family. For I am the shy candle, afraid to let my light shine.

# Have They Forgotten Us?

As Veterans Day approaches, there is a question that runs through my mind: Have they forgotten us? Have they forgotten all the hours that we trained side by side? Have they forgotten the many hours of training and the ones that out shown them in the training? Were there any that come to mind that took a bullet for her friend and was not sorry for the pain she went through? We are the few and the proud, the women of the Armed Forces of this great land.

There have been a few that have been on the news, and then they were put back into a corner somewhere and only shown when they wanted to makes points with the public. There are a few that have served that are acknowledged for their bravery and their sacrifice as mothers wives while still serving this country.

The old school Navy, Army, Marines, Air Force and Coast Guard: WAVES, WACS, WAFS, AND MARINES( nicknamed BAMS) these ladies and their counterparts in the new Army, Navy, Air Force and Marines have served their country and do not get the praise of the Nation like the men.

Could it be that we are lesser that the men? Or is it that the Nation dose not want to think about the weather have helped to keep this Nation free right beside their fellow male soldiers? When there is a Death of a soldier in a foreign land by a land mine, or in a fire fight, you never hear about the women whom went out to bring back the bodies or were injured. You hear about how brave the men were and that they are given metals of honor for their deeds. You do not hear about the females that were there in just as much danger as the men. There are a few that have been honored, but there are many more that are not even named as being in the troops that have gone in and brought out the heroes. Are they any less a hero for their work and sacrifices?

Have we forgotten our young women in arms that leave behind their children and other family members to keep us free from the terrors that they face daily?

Let us raise our voices and let it be known that we salute our sisters at arms. Let them know that they have not been forgotten and that they never will be. I know I will no forget you. Nora B. Montgomery (Former Army)

# Her Heart Beat Music

**The Bonnie Clemons Story As Seen Through The Eyes of Her Student**

**Nora B. Montgomery (Decker )**

## The Beginning

September, Nineteen sixty-three was the start of my fourth grade year at Kearney R-1 Elementary School. Mrs. Clemons was our new music teacher and we all loved her. She had a way of making you understand even the hardest parts of music and making it fun to learn. As a young student, I was one of the students that took to music like a duck to water and I could hardly wait for Music class. This was the year that we would learn to read music and start playing instruments. But first we had to learn to play the flute phone, now known recorder. I was so happy to be playing it that I practiced every night and all weekend so that I could make Mrs. Clemons smile. You might say that I had a need to make her happy with me, and did my best to do just that. That fall was a very traumatic for my family and me. We lost our home to fire and had to move into town for the winter. It was shortly after the first of the year in nineteen sixty-four that we picked out the instruments that we wanted to play in band. I can still remember that night when we were in the gymnasium of the school and there were tables set up with all kinds of instruments to look at. There were clarinets, flutes, trumpets, trombones, drums, French horns and baritones for us to chose from. I was drawn to the flute and I picked one up, put it together and nearly played a scale. I can still remember the salesman telling Mrs. Clemons and Mom that I was a natural. Mom and Dad got me that flute and Mrs. Clemons began teaching my classmates and myself Band. Like the flute-phone I took to the flute and practiced all the time. That was the beginning of my undying love for Mrs. Clemons and Music.

From the start of the fifth grade year, I could hardly wait for Band and Music classes. I wanted to spend as much time with Mrs. Clemons as I could. Music was my favorite class and she was my favorite teacher. I even made her a Mother's Day card, only to learn that she did not have any children. She thanked me anyway and told me that her students were the closest to children that she had. I cried because I thought I had made her sad but she smiled and gave me a hug for thinking of her that way. That year Mrs. Clemons became not just my teacher but also a friend.

The next year, when I was having problems with my other school work, she told me that if I did not get my grades up that she would have to drop me from band. That nearly broke my heart, so my grades improved. All of us Band students worked hard to make out concerts the very best they could be and we were eager to be rewarded by one of Mrs. Clemons loving smiles. We would practice our fingers sore to get a smile from her.

The summer between Sixth and Seventh grades, most of us were involved in the Summer Ban. We Started learning to march while playing our instruments and we even went to the State Fair to march there. That was the first year in the new Junior High building and Band room. We played with the High School Band and Marched with them too. That year, Mrs. Clemons completed her Masters in Music at Central Missouri State College. All the students got together and bought her a card and a present to show how proud of her we were. She was really taken by surprise and she cried knowing that we cared so much for her.

The next Summer we practiced marching getting ready for the football season. We marched in several parades and the next spring, the Junior High had a District Band contest. Two of the other flute players and myself made up a trio and played at contest. I also took a solo and got a one. Mrs. Clemons was so proud of us. We got a two that year but we were still happy that we had done so well. Mrs. Clemons was pleased and she had a Band picnic that year for all of us that played so well.

Mrs. Clemons was the heart and soul of our music department, and it did not make any difference if you were in band or in the chorus, she could bring out the music in you. She not only expected the best of your, but of herself as well. That is what made her so good at what she did. I can remember the long hours that she put in at school helping out students that took solos to contest and the other groups as well. In fact, she spent many hours with us practicing for marching programs, concerts, and contests. She was always encouraging and very seldom raised her voice to her students. I can only remember twice that I ever saw her truly mad and that was when two of the boys in the band started fighting and nearly broke one of the instruments. Her love of music was contagious and she passed it on to her students. There not one of her students that did not have a love of music and did not do their very best to please her. Her summer Band classes were attended by almost all of her band students, and it did not seem as hot when we were practicing as it did otherwise.

My Freshman year started off happy and full of hope for a great year of being part of the High School. Band, of course, was my best class and I practiced all the time so that I could challenge for a better chair in the flute section. That year I challenged up to third chair. There were only two Seniors ahead of me and I was very happy about that. Mrs. Clemons said that he was proud of me and I worked hard to keep my teacher happy.

That years marching, practices, and concerts until Christmas break were filled with a lot of Mrs. Clemons smiles and we knew that she was proud of us. We were looking forward to contest and I had planned to take a solo in hopes of another one.

The day after Christmas, nineteen sixty-nine, is a day that will remain a sad day for the Music Department at Kearney R-1. Mrs. Clemons, out beloved teacher, had been killed in a car wreck the night before, leaving us all in a state of shock and disbelief. I know that I cried for two days and it took going to her funeral to accept that she was truly gone. She had not only been my teacher but also my mentor. Her love of music and her ability to bring out the music in me made me strive to be like her. At her funeral I did pretty well until her husband clutching her picture said. "Bonnie, Babe, I tried to miss them but I couldn't. I'm sorry". There was not a dry eye in the church as we said good bye to the Heart and Soul of a beautiful and gracious lady that had come to mean so much to all her students. Her heart came out in her music and it took hold of the hearts of her students as well. Her heart beat music.

It was hard for her students to go back too school and not see her smiling face in a the music room. It was even harder to accept the new music teacher that came in to take her place. He was a good teacher but he could never take the place of Mrs. Clemons in our hearts.

Bonnie Lou Clemons, you were and always will be , the teacher that kept this music student in school in honor of your memory. I not only was your student but I loved you with all my young heart. The music that lives in me was planted and nurtured by you. Your memory lives in my heart and in my music.

# The Antique Doll

Sitting in the corner on a high chair, sat Annabelle, an antique china doll. She had been sitting there in the corner waiting for her mistress to come play with her. It had been a long time since her mistress had played with her and she was getting very sad. Annabelle noticed that many of the other toys that mistress played with, were also just sitting in the place where they had been put away.

One night, Annabelle ask the teddy bear on the stool near by if he knew where the mistress was. Teddy was just as puzzled by the absence of the mistress as Annabelle. Quietly, she ask the other toys if they had seen the mistress. All gave the same answer. No one had seen the mistress for a long time and they too were very sad.

Every few days the maid would come in and dust the room and make sure that they were kept clean, but there was no sigh of the mistress. One day, the maid pulled the blinds and placed sheets over all the furniture and looked sadly around the room. Then she shut the door.

Several days went by and the maid did not come back in to dust, and the toys began to worry that they had been forgotten and that they would not ever see the mistress again. Weeks and months passed turning into years and still, there was no sign of the mistress.

Many years had passed with Annabelle and the toys under the sheets that the maid had placed over them. When one day, the door to the room creaked open and a dim light was cast over the room. Annabelle and the toys sat wondering if the mistress had finally returned.

They were shocked when a man in a business suit and a lady in a dark dress looked under the sheets to see what was there. This was not the mistress or the lady that had taken care of them so long ago. Where was the mistress? Had she forgotten them? They were all quiet and listened carefully as the lady and man went around the room talking.

When the lady came to the corner where Annabelle was sitting, she was surprised to see such a lovely doll. She gently picked Annabelle up and looked her over. Turning to the man she explained that Annabelle was

A real find that there were very few dolls like her left. None that she had seen were of the quality of Annabelle and that Annabelle was a real prize find. She would bring top dollar at the auction.

This made Annabelle very glad that she would soon be with another mistress, but she still wondered what had happened to her old one.

Later that day, a lady came in. She cleaned and dusted the room, and talked to the toys saying,`` Some lucky child will have some very nice toys indeed." When she got to the corner where Annabelle sat, tears came to her eyes and she gently took her in her arms, and rocked her the way the mistress had all those many years before. She whispered softly to Annabelle that she, in her childhood, had a doll much like Annabelle except that her doll had blonde hair where Annabelle had red hair. Her doll had been dressed in a blue velvet dress and had a parasol that matched, where Annabelle was dressed in dark green velvet with a matching hat. The lady wrapped Annabelle in a soft cloth and placed her in a box so that she would not be broken in the move from the room to the auction house. All the other toys were wrapped and put in boxes too.

Laying in the box waiting for the day of the auction, Annabelle wondered what was to happen to all the mistresses toys, would they all be together or would they never see each other again? On the morning of the auction, Annabelle and the other toys were put out on display for the people to see. Much to their surprise, there were no children at the auction, only big people like the lady and man that had come to the room all those days ago.

People came around looking at the toys, but Annabelle seemed to be getting the most attention. Many of the ladies in the auction house were coming by to examine her and commenting on how beautiful she was. They stated that she was in excellent condition and an extraordinary find.

There was one lady that kept coming back to look at Annabelle. There was something about her that kept the lady coming back over and over. The lady was in her late thirties or early forties. There was something that kept nagging at her about this doll. In the back of her mind there was a story about a doll that fit the description of Annabelle.

According to the story, her grandmother had once had a doll that was left in the grandmothers room when she was taken away to live with her grandparents and she never saw it again. Her grandmother was now near ninety and often spoke of the porcelain doll with the auburn hair and big blue eyes dressed in the green velvet dress and hat that matched. Could this be that doll? She had come to this auction because the things were from the house that had been on the property that had once belonged to her great-grandparents, and according to the papers, the room where this doll was found had once belonged to a little girl. If this doll did not to too high, the lady was going to buy it and make it a present for her Grandmothers birthday.

As the bidding started, the lady that had found Annabelle told the crowd about the doll and where she had been found. One lady started the bidding at one hundred dollars. Another, bid one hundred fifty and on it went until the lady that wanted the doll for her Grandmother called out five hundred fifty dollars. The auctioneer called once, twice, sold for five hundred fifty dollars to the lady in the back. ``Please pay the cashier and this lovely little lady is yours."

Annabelle was once again wrapped up and placed in a box. She was taken to the ladies home. She was cleaned, and carefully rewrapped with a new blanket, and them taken to the ladies grandmother.

When the old lady unwrapped Annabelle, she gave a gasp of sheer delight at the sight of the doll. The first thing she did was turn her upside down and look under the dolls heavy skirt at the body of the doll. There, in small neat letters, was the name Annabelle and the date January 25, 1895. Big tears of joy ran down her cheeks as she read the name and date out loud to her gathered family. Then she said,`` Annabelle, dear Annabelle, I have you once again."

She turned to her granddaughter and asked, ``where did you find her? I can hardly believe my old eyes but here she is, my darling Annabelle, after all these years." Carefully and lovingly, she wrapped the doll in The new blanket and held her as she told the story of the night she and her mother left the house never to return. The doll, Annabelle, had been her mother's doll when she was a girl and she had given it to her daughter on her fifth birthday. This was eighty five years before. It had been hard to leave the doll behind but there had been little she could do under the circumstances and she had always hoped that Annabelle would be taken care of by whoever found her. Never dreaming that one day Annabelle would find her way back to her arms. Only a few short weeks later, the old lady passed away and Annabelle was given back to the young lady that had lovingly given her grandmother so much joy in her last days. Now Annabelle sits in a glass case with many new friends that have stories much like hers.

Dolls of all sizes lovingly given to little girls by their grandmothers all those years ago and now, housed where many can enjoy them.

Epilogue

This collection of poems and prose started as therapy but has become a passion that I hope to continue for many more years. Hopefully you have enjoyed them. There is a smile written in these pages and I hope you smiled too.

# About the Author

Nora Decker Montgomery lives in the Northwest area of Missouri with her husband of twenty-eight years and their dog Sadie and cat Smokey. Nora started writing as a release. She likes to write what comes to mind in the form of poems and prose. She has been writing on and off for the last twenty years, but this is her first book. She has been published in the *Veterans Voice*, a magazine of poems and prose written by veterans that are in the hospital for therapy. Nora is an Army veteran, and her husband is a Navy veteran. Nora enjoys being outdoors and fishing for catfish with her husband. She would love to hear from you at ladymunchkin184@ yahoo.com.